P

A collection of d_____ ___ make recipes

Contents

Text by James Phillips.

Originally published in 2009 by L&K Designs. This edition published in 2010 by Myriad Books Limited
© L&K Designs 2009
PRINTED IN CHINA

Publishers Disclaimer

The recipes contained in this book are passed on in good faith but the publisher cannot be held responsible for any adverse results. Please be aware that certain recipes may contain nuts.

For many years now, pasta has been an integral part of most people's diets. Whilst connoisseurs of pasta will have you believe that fresh pasta is the only choice, dried pasta is a quicker alternative, and just as delicious!

Many households search for economical foods which are healthy for their families, and also taste great. Pasta fits that bill superbly as it is virtually salt and fat free, in addition to having a low Glycemic Index (GI).

Pasta is a complex carbohydrate, which should constitute a higher percentage of your diet. It is digested more slowly than other foods, meaning that it naturally satisfies hunger for longer, without spiking blood sugar levels. Facts state that 1/2 cup of cooked pasta contains a mere 99 calories, meaning you can enjoy delicious pasta-based recipes without worrying about piling on the pounds - it is the sauces which can cause problems!

Unfortunately, the origin of pasta still remains a grey area in history. There are many theories circulating, one stating that Marco Polo brought it back to Italy whilst exploring the Far East, while Greek Mythology suggests that Vulcan, the Greek God of fire, created the first machine to turn dough into long thin strands (spaghetti).

Dried pasta is made in four easy steps - mixing, extruding, drying and then packing.

Firstly, a hard wheat (usually semolina) is mixed with water to form a dough. Then the dough is kneaded, and extruded through a machine to create its shape (different shaped machines create our uniquely shaped pasta today).

After this, the pasta sheets are sent through dryers which circulate hot air, speeding up the process. Finally, the dried pasta is packed into boxes or bags, and distributed to shops all over the world!

Many people fret about cooking the 'perfect' pasta, but if you follow these simple instructions, you won't go far wrong! Once you've got this mastered, simply complete the rest of your recipe, and you'll have a delicious pasta-based meal!

1. Boil 4 litres of water for every 450g of dry pasta (1 litre per 110g - you can divide this recipe depending on how much pasta you are cooking.)

2. Add the pasta with a stir and return the water to a boil. Stir the pasta occasionally during cooking.

3. Follow the package directions for cooking times. If the pasta is to be used as part of a dish that requires further cooking, undercook the pasta by 1/3 of the cooking time specified on the package.

4. Taste the pasta to determine if it is done. Perfectly cooked pasta should be "al dente," or firm to the bite, yet cooked through.

5. Drain pasta immediately and follow the rest of the recipe.

When cooking with dried pasta, there are many different varieties available, but some are much more commonly used than others. Here is a list of the pastas which are most popular today, how to identify them and what they are best served with.

Bucatini

Bucatini is a thick spaghetti-like pasta with a hole running through the centre. The name comes from buco, meaning "hole" in Italian. It is usually served with buttery sauces, eggs, and anchovies or sardines.

Cannelloni

Cannelloni are large tubular shaped pasta pieces that are usually filled with either a sauce (bolognaise or vegetable-based) or meat. For a regular sized meal, each person would usually be served with 4-6 cannelloni each.

Capellini

Capellini is similar to spaghetti, although the long ribbon-like pieces are slightly thicker, and hollowed out in the middle. It is often used as a substitute to spaghetti, as it takes much less time to cook. It is a great pasta when served with a pesto sauce, but is often used with bolognaise.

Farfalle

Farfalle is one of the most popular pastas especially with children, due to its shape. Shaped like butterflies or bow-ties (after the Italian word "farfalla", meaning butterfly), it is most commonly used with a tomato sauce, although it's known to be used in pasta salads, largely due to its appealing shape.

Fettuccine

Named after the Italian word for "little ribbons", fettuccine is a long, thin pasta resembling ribbons. Strands of fettuccine are usually between 5 and 7mm thick. It is sometimes mistaken for tagliatelle, but fettuccine is much thicker.

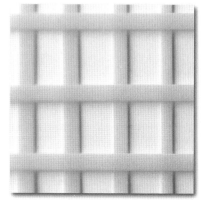

Fusilli Lunghi

Fusilli lunghi are large spiral shaped pasta pieces, similar to that of penne pasta, but usually much thicker and slightly longer. It is most commonly used in pasta bakes, with rich and creamy sauces, and with cheese-based pasta dishes.

Gnocchi

Gnocchi is an Italian-style potato dumpling, usually oval shaped, and are served with a sauce - much like regular pasta shapes. There is also a type of pasta called gnocchi, to the confusion of many, which are shell-shaped. Tomato and cheese based sauces go well with gnocchi.

Lasagne

Lasagne are sheets of pasta and is most commonly used in the dish, which goes by the same name. The dish is easy to make, due to the sheets of lasagne placed in between layers of meat and cheese. Lasagne all'uovo is an alternative, which contains egg, and has a richer flavour than classic lasagne.

Linguine

Linguine is another long, thin pasta, and resembles flat spaghetti. The name "Linguine" comes from the Italian meaning "Little Tongues". It is best served with a rich sauce, which will cling to the pasta, and with seafood or other meat mixed in.

Macaroni

Macaroni is a machine-made dry pasta, and is famous for its popularity in macaroni and cheese dishes. They are identified as U-shaped tubes. To make macaroni cheese, just cover the pasta in a cheesy (usually cheddar) sauce, but other creamy sauces can be used instead.

Nidi vermicelli

Nidi vermicelli, Italian for small worms, are smaller and thinner strands of spaghetti. Be wary when cooking with nidi vermicellii, as thin sauces are recommended. Any heavy sauces will soak into the pasta and cause it to go soggy.

Penne

Penne pasta is one of the most instantly recognisable pastas around. With most individual strands being 3-5cm hollow tubes, diagonally cut at each end, penne is an all-time favourite, usually served in pasta bakes, but also works well with heavier sauces and cheesy sauces too.

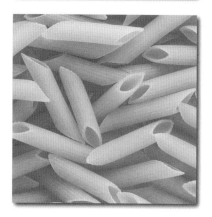

Ravioli

Ravioli usually takes the form of a square but sometimes comes in a circular variety. It is often filled with cheese, but there are varieties stuffed with either meat, vegetables or a mixture of the two.

Rigatoni

Rigatoni is a form of tube-shaped pasta. It is larger than penne and ziti. Rigatoni is usually ridged and the tube's end does not finish at an angle, like penne. Rigatoni can be coupled with many different sauces, from creamy to chunky, and can sometimes be stuffed with cheese or other soft foods.

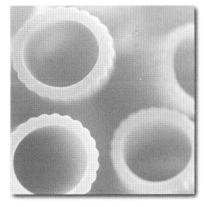

Spaghetti

Spaghetti is probably the most common pasta to be eaten worldwide. It is a long, worm-like strand of pasta which is very thin. It is often eaten with bolognaise and carbonara dishes.

Tagliatelle

Tagliatelle is a thin ribbon-like pasta. It's name comes from "tagliare" which means "to cut" in Italian. Tagliatelle comes in a "tricolore" version too, with white pasta, tomato-flavoured red pasta and spinach-flavoured green strands. When using the tricolore pasta, use pale sauces to bring out the colours.

Ziti

Similar in shape to penne pasta, ziti are medium sized, tubular strands of pasta, hollowed out through the middle. The difference between ziti and penne is the thickness, with ziti being slightly thinner. Ziti is best served with pasta bakes and light sauces, as thicker sauces can drown the pasta.

Storing pasta is relatively easy, even when you've cooked your pasta. Store uncooked pasta in a cupboard, or on a shelf, but make sure it is out of direct sunlight. It can be stored uncooked for up to a year.

Cooked pasta can be stored in the fridge for 3 or 4 days, and the best way to stop it from sticking in a bowl is to add a drop of olive oil.

And pasta can also be frozen, although the best shapes to freeze are those used in pasta bakes. Prepare the dish as per instructions, then thaw to room temperature before cooking, and bake as the recipe directs.

It is a good idea to stock most of the commonly used pastas in your house - many people have not tried the different types of pasta, but once you start using all of the different varieties available, you'll be amazed at just how versatile pasta really is!

Spice things up for kids by buying coloured pastas shapes, or even specialized shapes which are available in supermarkets, of cartoon characters. It generally helps a child enjoy their meal if it has a unique and colourful appearance, so always make it look appetizing for the child.

Pasta is a big favourite for dieters as a lunch time snack. For anybody on a diet, pasta and tuna, prepared the day before, is the perfect recipe.

One of the most important things to do when using pasta is to make sure you have the right shapes with the right sauces and dishes.

When using flat or thin spaghetti, thinner sauces should be used, as you may risk drowning your pasta in the sauce. Tubular, and more dense pasta is recommended for thicker sauces.

But this doesn't mean you have to stick to the same pasta - why not try out your own recipes? And if they work really well, write them down in the space at the back of this book!

Chicken Tarragon Tagliatelle (Serves 2) ✳

Ingredients

255g/2 1/2 cups tagliatelle pasta
2 garlic cloves, chopped
2 skinless chicken breast fillets, cut into small pieces
2 tbsps olive oil
100g/1/2 cup spinach leaves, thick stems removed
150ml/3/4 cup single cream
3 tbsps fresh tarragon leaves, roughly chopped
Salt and freshly ground black pepper
Lemon wedges, to serve

Method

1. Pour the pasta into a large saucepan. Cook the pasta in a large pan of boiling water for 8-10 minutes, or according to packet instructions, until just tender.

2. Whilst you cook the pasta, heat the oil in a frying pan, then add the chicken and fry over a high heat for 4-5 minutes until cooked, stirring every minute or so.

3. Add the garlic to the frying pan, then stir in the tarragon, cream and 3 tablespoons of the pasta cooking liquid. Heat through over a low heat.

4. When the pasta is cooked, put the spinach into the same pan and stir well (it will wilt in the hot water). Drain the spinach and pasta mixture well, then toss into the creamy chicken.

Season with salt and pepper, then serve with lemon wedges on the side for squeezing.

Chicken, Bacon & Basil Pasta (Serves 1) ✳

Ingredients

125g/1 1/4 cups farfalle pasta (cooked)
2 rashers bacon (chopped)
1 boneless chicken thigh (skin removed, cut into strips)
1 garlic clove, crushed
240ml/1 cup double cream
1 tbsp olive oil
Sprinkle of salt
Sprinkle of freshly ground black pepper
85g/1/2 cup cheddar (grated) (plus extra to garnish)

Method

1. Heat the olive oil in a frying pan, add the chicken strips and bacon and cook for 4-5 minutes, or until the chicken is cooked through.

2. Add the garlic and cook for 1 minute. Season with salt and freshly ground black pepper, add the cream and warm through.

3. Add the creamy sauce to the cooked, drained pasta and stir well. To serve, add the basil and cheddar, mix and spoon onto a serving plate. Garnish with extra grated cheese and basil leaves if desired.

Sausage and Penne Rigate (Serves 4)

Ingredients

75g/1/3 cup butter
4 pork sausages
375g/3 1/2 cups dried penne rigate pasta
75g/3/4 cup freshly grated parmesan cheese
1 garlic clove (peeled and chopped)
1 small onion (peeled and chopped)
1 sprig rosemary (finely chopped)
1 tbsp ground cloves
160ml/3/4 cup dry white wine
Pinch of freshly grated nutmeg
Pinch of salt
Sprinkle of freshly ground black pepper

Method

1. Heat the butter and gently fry the garlic and the onion. Remove the skin from the sausages and chop them up into equal pieces.

2. Add to the pan and slowly fry until well browned. Add the rosemary with the wine, and cook gently for 10 minutes. Add the cloves, nutmeg, salt and pepper.

3. Meanwhile, cook the pasta until al dente, and drain. Mix with the sausage mixture and serve with parmesan cheese sprinkled over.

Bacon & Pumpkin Pesto Pasta (Serves 4)

Ingredients

1 pumpkin (approximately 1kg - deseeded, peeled, cut into small pieces)
400g/4 cups dried penne pasta
6 rashers streaky bacon (chopped into squares)
1 tbsp olive oil
Salt & freshly ground black pepper
125g/1/2 cup pesto sauce
Parmesan shavings (to serve)

Method

1. Preheat oven to 200C/400F/Gas Mark 6. Line a baking tray with non-stick cooking paper. Place the pumpkin, in a single layer, on the prepared tray. Drizzle with olive oil and season with salt and pepper. Bake in oven for 25 minutes or until tender.

2. Whilst the pumpkin cooks, place the pasta in a large saucepan of salted boiling water and cook until al dente. Drain and return to the pan.

3. Cook the bacon in a large frying pan over medium-high heat, stirring, for 5 minutes or until crisp and golden.

4. Add the pesto sauce to the pasta and toss well, until coated. Add the pumpkin and bacon and mix until well combined.

Serve immediately with the parmesan shavings.

Creamy Bacon & Egg Linguine (Serves 4)
Ingredients

12 thin bacon rashers (cut into thin strips)
400g/3 1/2 cups linguine
300ml/1 1/3 cup thickened cream
4 eggs
1 garlic clove (finely chopped)
2 tbsps parsley leaves (finely chopped)
1 tbsp olive oil
100g/1 cup grated parmesan (plus extra to serve)

Method

1. Heat the olive oil in a large pan over a medium heat. Add the bacon and stir for 4 minutes, or until crisp. Remove to a plate, then set the pan to one side.

2. Meanwhile, cook the linguine in a large saucepan of boiling salted water according to packet instructions. Drain, leaving the pasta in a colander, and return the pasta pan to a low heat.

3. Add the cream, garlic and half the bacon and warm through for 2 minutes. Return the pasta to the pan and mix well, to coat. Set aside, cover and keep warm.

4. Return the bacon pan to the stove over a medium heat. Crack the eggs into the pan, and fry for 2 minutes until the whites are firm but the yolks are still runny.

5. Stir the grated parmesan through the pasta with half the parsley. Season with pepper. Divide the pasta into 4 medium bowls, then top each with an egg.

Serve sprinkled with remaining bacon and parsley, and extra parmesan.

Cheese, Ham & Broccoli Penne (Serves 4) ✳

Ingredients

375g/3 3/4 cups dried penne pasta
6 slices of double-smoked ham, chopped
450g/5 cups broccoli, cut into small florets
2 egg yolks
170ml/3/4 cup light evaporated milk
75g/3/4 cup grated parmesan
2 garlic cloves, crushed
3 green onions, chopped
1 tbsp olive oil

Method

1. In a large saucepan of salted water, cook the pasta until tender, adding the broccoli for the last 3 minutes of cooking, and drain.

2. Heat the olive oil in a large frying pan over a high heat. Add the garlic, ham and onion. Cook for 2 to 3 minutes whilst stirring continuously or until onion has softened. Add pasta and broccoli, then reduce the heat to low.

3. Whisk the milk, cheese and egg yolks together in a small jug. Add to the pasta, and season with salt and pepper. Stir briefly, then cook for 2 to 3 minutes or until heated through, then serve.

Turkey & Linguine Saute (Serves 6)

Ingredients

450g/4 cups linguine
2 cups diced & cooked turkey
1/4 cup herbed stuffing mix
2 celery stalks (diced)
1 large onion (diced)
1 cup chicken broth
2 cups broccoli florets
2 carrots (thinly sliced)
2 tbsps all-purpose flour
1 tbsp butter
1 tsp ground sage

Turkey & Linguine Saute/cont.
Method

1. Prepare the pasta according to package directions, and cook until al dente. Two minutes before the pasta is done, add broccoli florets to water. Cook for the remaining two minutes, then drain the pasta and broccoli.

2. In a large pan, warm the butter over a medium heat. Add the onion, carrots and celery and saute for three minutes. Stir in the flour, add the chicken broth and sage and stir in the turkey. Stir until the sauce comes to a simmer, then allow to simmer for 1 minute.

3. Pour the turkey saute over the pasta. Sprinkle the stuffing mix on top and serve immediately.

Barbequed Chicken Pasta (Serves 4)
Ingredients

285g/2 cups rigatoni (uncooked)
2 boneless, skinless chicken breasts (cubed)
40g/1/4 cup green bell pepper (thinly sliced)
40g/1/4 cup red onion (thinly sliced)
60ml/1/4 cup barbeque sauce
85g/1/2 cup provolone cheese (grated)
80g/1/2 cup gouda cheese (grated)
115ml/1/2 cup tomato sauce
1 tbsp vegetable oil
1 tsp garlic (finely chopped)
3 scallions, trimmed and sliced thin
1/4 cup whole cilantro (flat leaf parsley) leaves

Method

1. Prepare pasta according to package directions and cook until al dente. Meanwhile, heat oil in a large pan over a medium heat. Add the chicken and sauté, stirring occasionally, until browned on all sides.

2. Add the bell pepper, garlic and onion and cook for 1-2 minutes. Add tomato sauce and barbeque sauce and heat just to boiling, then remove from the heat.

3. Drain the pasta, reserving 1/4 cup of water and return pasta to the pot. Add chicken mixture and cheese to the pot. Stir over a low heat until pasta is coated well with sauce.

4. Add enough of reserved cooking liquid, if necessary, to make the sauce lightly coat the pasta. Transfer pasta to a serving bowl and top with scallions and cilantro.

Mexican-Style Macaroni (Serves 2-4)

Ingredients

225g/1 1/2 cups macaroni (uncooked)
225g/1 1/2 cups ground beef
120ml/1/2 cup medium salsa
1 small green bell pepper (chopped)
400g/2 1/2 cups kidney beans (drained)
2 medium tomatoes (seeded and chopped)
225ml/1 cup low-fat yoghurt
80g/1/2 cup Cheddar cheese (grated)
1 green onion (sliced)
100g/1/2 cup broken tortilla chips
1 tsp chilli powder
1/2 tsp ground cumin

Method

1. Prepare the pasta according to package directions, and cook until al dente, then drain.

2. In a medium pan, brown the ground beef and drain well. Add the kidney beans, chilli powder and cumin, and heat through.

3. In a large bowl, combine the pasta, meat mixture, tomatoes, cheese, green pepper and onions. In a small bowl, combine the yoghurt and salsa.

4. Mix well, then serve warm or cold.

Garnish with tortilla chips and serve with additional salsa.

Mandarin Chicken & Pasta Salad (Serves 6)

Ingredients

220g/1 cup farfalle pasta
2 tomatoes (diced)
1 carrot (shredded)
170g/1 cup fresh spinach
4 boneless chicken breasts (cooked & chopped)
1/2 tsp root ginger
80ml/1/3 cup vinegar
60ml/1/4 cup orange juice
60ml/1/4 cup vegetable oil
1 tsp toasted sesame oil
1 packet dry onion soup mix
2 tsps white sugar
1 garlic clove
1 small cucumber (seeded, and sliced)
2 red bell peppers (diced)
1 red onion (chopped)
3 tbsps sliced almonds, toasted

Method

1. To make the dressing, whisk together the root ginger, vinegar, orange juice, vegetable oil, sesame oil, soup mix, garlic and sugar until well blended. Cover, and refrigerate until needed.

2. Bring a large pot of lightly salted water to a boil. Add the farfalle pasta and cook until al dente then drain and rinse under cold water. Place pasta in a large bowl.

3. To make the salad, toss the cucumber, bell pepper, onion, tomatoes, carrot, spinach, chicken, and almonds with the pasta. Pour the dressing over the salad mixture, and toss again to coat evenly.

Serve immediately.

Ham & Apple Pasta in Cider Sauce (Serves 4)

Sauce Ingredients

290ml/1 1/3 cups dry cider
290ml/1 1/3 cups chicken stock
150ml/2/3 cup double cream
2 tbsps butter
2 tbsps plain flour
Salt and freshly ground black pepper

Pasta Ingredients

340g/3 cups penne pasta
3 red eating apples
225g/1 1/2 cups good quality ham
2 tbsps butter
4 tsps brown sugar
2 peppers (sliced)

Method

1. For the sauce, heat the butter in a saucepan and gradually add the flour. Cook for 2 minutes over a medium heat, but do not allow it to colour.

2. Remove from the heat. Slowly add the stock and cider. Stir between each addition to ensure sauce is of a smooth consistency.

3. When half the liquid is added, return the pan to the heat and slowly bring to the boil. As it begins to thicken add the rest of the liquid. Allow to boil for at least 2 minutes.

4. Meanwhile, bring a pan of water to the boil. Cook the pasta until al dente. Slice the ham into finger-length slices and set aside.

5. Chop the apples into wedges. Melt the butter in a small pan and add the brown sugar. Let it almost caramelise and then fry the apple wedges.

6. Drain the pasta and add to the sauce, before adding the ham, apples and peppers. Season with salt and pepper.

Ham & Apple Pasta in Cider Sauce/cont.

7. Reheat thoroughly and serve. (Note: If you do need to keep this dish hot for a while add a little more stock or water. Mix in most of the apples and put in an ovenproof dish, cover with tin foil and place in the oven at 140C/275F/Gas Mark 1)

Spicy Chorizo & Tomato Pasta (Serves 4)

Ingredients

450g/4 cups penne pasta
16 fresh ripe tomatoes (peeled, seeded and diced)
4 chorizo sausages
150ml/2/3 cup single cream
2 tbsps butter
3 tbsps flat leaf parsley (finely chopped)
4 tbsps freshly grated parmesan
1 tsp finely chopped rosemary
1 tsp crushed chillies
Pinch of sugar

Method

1. Melt the butter in a saucepan, add the chopped rosemary and diced tomatoes. Season with salt and pepper and sugar.

2. Cook until the tomatoes have just begun to soften into a sauce, which takes about 5 minutes.

3. Slice the sausages and add to the pan with the crushed chillies. Add the cream and 2 tbsps of chopped flat leaf parsley, and allow to bubble for 3-4 minutes, stirring frequently until the cream has reduced by half.

4. Remove the pan from the heat and set aside. Cook the pasta until al dente, drain and toss with the sauce, then add the grated parmesan.

Serve with remaining parsley.

Lemon Pork Pasta (Serves 4)

Ingredients

6 sausages
1 lemon
1 tbsp dried chilli flakes
210ml/1 cup crème fraiche
450g/4 cups penne pasta
4 tbsps frozen peas
Parmesan shavings

Method

1. Take the sausages and split the skins, squeezing the meat from each sausage into a hot pan. Pan-fry, breaking up the meat, until golden and crispy in places.

2. Add the grated lemon zest, a good squeeze of lemon juice, dried chilli flakes and crème fraiche. Boil for 1 minute.

3. Cook pasta until al dente. Add the peas to the water for the last 2 minutes. Drain, reserving some of the cooking water.

4. Toss the pasta and peas with the sauce, thinning down with the cooking water as necessary.

Serve with lots of freshly grated Parmesan.

Gammon & Garlic Pasta (Serves 4)
Ingredients
400g/3 1/2 cups farfalle pasta
1 large piece of gammon (roughly chopped)
5 garlic cloves (peeled and left whole)
200g/1 1/2 cups spinach (washed)
3 tbsps creme fraiche
2 tbsps butter
1 tbsp olive oil
1 tsp black pepper
Parmesan shavings

Method
1. Cook the pasta in boiling water according to packet instructions, until al dente. Meanwhile, cook the garlic in a pan of boiling water until tender.

2. Drain and toss into a large non-stick frying pan with the butter and olive oil and cook over a low heat until golden.

3. Add the spinach and cook until it begins to wilt, whilst adding a few tablespoons of creme fraiche and the chopped gammon.

4. Bring up to the boil, season with pepper and toss into the cooked pasta.

Serve in a bowl with grated parmesan.

Chicken & Red Pepper Pesto Pasta (Serves 2)
Ingredients
2 chicken breast fillets (chopped)
3 tbsps roasted red pepper pesto
250g/9 oz pasta of your choice
1 tbsp olive oil
1 tbsp salted water
2 courgettes (sliced)
4 tbsps green beans
350g/3 cups mascarpone cheese
Parmesan shavings

Method

1. Heat the oil in a medium-sized pan and cook the chicken for 3-4 minutes until browned.

2. Add the courgettes and beans and cook for 3-4 minutes until softened.

3. In a separate bowl, mix together the roasted red pepper pesto and the mascarpone cheese. Pour the sauce into the pan and simmer gently for 5 minutes, stirring every now and again.

4. Meanwhile, cook the pasta until al dente. Drain the pasta well and then stir into the sauce.

5. Finally spoon the pasta into the serving bowls.

Serve with parmesan shavings sprinkled over the top.

Bacon & Broccoli Linguine (Serves 2-3)
Ingredients
200g/2 cups linguine (cooked until al dente)
1/2 onion (chopped)
4 rashers bacon (chopped)
1/4 of a broccoli (cut into florets)
1 tbsp olive oil
3 free-range eggs (lightly beaten)
Salt and freshly ground black pepper

Method
1. Heat the oil in a small frying pan and fry the bacon until crisp. Add the onion and fry until softened.

2. Add the broccoli and fry for 3-4 minutes, stirring frequently, until softened. Add the linguine to the pan. Season the eggs with salt and freshly ground black pepper and pour into the pan.

3. Cook over a medium heat until the base is set and golden-brown, then carefully cover the frying pan with a plate and turn the frittata out onto the plate.

4. Slide the frittata back into the pan and cook until browned on the other side. To serve, cut the frittata into wedges and place onto serving plates.

Spicy Bacon & Pepper Pasta (Serves 1-2)
Ingredients
2 cloves garlic (chopped)
150g/1 1/2 cups penne pasta (cooked until al dente)
3 rashers streaky bacon (chopped)
1 red pepper (chopped)
1/4 leek (chopped)
1 tbsp olive oil
1 tbsp chilli flakes
Salt and freshly ground black pepper
Handful of basil (chopped)

Method

1. Heat the oil in a frying pan over a medium heat. Add the bacon and fry for 2-3 minutes.

2. Add the red pepper, garlic, leek and chilli flakes and season well with salt and freshly ground black pepper.

3. Cook gently for 3-4 minutes, then add a splash of boiling water and stir well. Stir in the cooked pasta and basil and immediately pour into a bowl and serve.

Chicken Carbonara (Serves 1)

Ingredients

1 skinless chicken breast
85g/3/4cup fettucine pasta (cooked until al dente, and drained)
55g/1/3 cup buffalo mozzarella (chopped)
100ml/1/2 cup double cream
4 tbsps white wine
1 tbsp olive oil
Handful fresh basil leaves (chopped)
Salt and freshly ground black pepper

Method

1. Cover the chicken breast with cling film and flatten out to 5mm/1/4-inch thick using a rolling pin.

2. Remove the cling film, then sprinkle the mozzarella pieces and half of the basil along the middle of the chicken.

3. Season with salt and freshly ground black pepper, then roll up to enclose the filling. Wrap tightly in cling film.

4. Place the chicken roll into a pan of simmering water and poach for 8-10 minutes, or until just cooked through.

5. Meanwhile, place the wine in a pan with the cream and simmer until reduced by one third. Season, to taste, with salt and freshly ground black pepper and stir in the remaining basil.

Roast Chicken Carbonara/cont.

6. Remove the chicken roll from the water and remove the cling film. Heat the olive oil in a pan and add the chicken roll. Fry gently for 3 minutes, turning regularly until golden-brown and completely cooked through.

7. Remove from the heat and leave to rest in a warm place. Add the cooked pasta to the pan of cream mixture and stir to coat.

To serve, place the pasta on a warmed plate. Cut the chicken into slices and arrange on top of the pasta.

Creamy Salmon Pasta (Serves 1)

Ingredients

75g/1/2 cup fresh salmon, cubed

150g/1 cup penne pasta (cooked)

2 tbsps olive oil

1 garlic clove, chopped

1/2 red onion, sliced

125ml/1/2 cup double cream

1 tbsp chopped fresh parsley

Method

1. Heat a medium-sized frying pan and add the oil, red onion and garlic. Sauté for 2 minutes, until the onion has softened.

2. Add the salmon cubes and double cream and continue to cook for five minutes, or until the salmon has cooked through.

3. Add to the pasta and stir before adding the parsley. Serve with parsley on the side too.

Scallop & Spaghetti Surprise (Serves 1)

Ingredients

4 scallops, sliced

110g/3/4 cup fresh spaghetti (cooked)

1 garlic clove (peeled and crushed)

1/4 red pepper (diced)

Zest & juice of 1 lemon

3 spring onions (chopped)

1 tbsp olive oil

Splash of champagne

2 tbsps olive oil (to serve)

2 slices of ciabatta (to serve)

Method

1. Heat the olive oil in a frying pan and saute the garlic and pepper for 5-6 minutes until softened. Add the champagne with the lemon juice and zest.

Scallop & Spaghetti Surprise/cont.

2. Stir in the sliced scallops and spring onions and heat until the scallops are cooked through. Stir in the cooked pasta and mix in with the sauce.

3. To serve, heat the oil in a non-stick griddle pan and chargrill the ciabatta slices for 2-3 minutes on each side until golden. Transfer the pasta to a bowl and serve with the grilled bread.

Garlic Prawn Pasta (Serves 4)

Ingredients

20 green prawns (peeled, deveined, tails intact)
230ml/1 cup white wine
500g/3 1/2 cups farfalle pasta
3 garlic cloves (crushed)
100g/2/3 cup unsalted butter
2 tbsps chopped fresh parsley
1 tbsp olive oil
1 tbsp capers
1/4 tsp dried red chilli flakes
Juice and zest of 1 large lemon

Method

1. In a large saucepan of salted water, cook the pasta until al dente. Drain, and return to the pan and toss with a little extra olive oil. Set aside to keep warm.

2. Place the remaining olive oil and the garlic in a frypan and heat gently over low heat. When the oil is hot, add the chilli flakes, prawns and half the parsley, increase heat to high and cook for 3 minutes.

3. Remove the prawns and set aside, then add the lemon juice and white wine to the pan and allow to reach close to boiling, then reduce the heat for 2 minutes.

4. Stir in the cold butter, lemon zest and capers until you have a smooth sauce. Return the prawns to the pan to heat through, then add the pasta.

Mix together well and serve garnished with the remaining parsley.

Tuna Macaroni Salad (Serves 1-2)

Ingredients

315g/1 1/2 cups macaroni
115g/1/2 cup sour cream
1 x 150g can of tuna (drained)
80ml/1/3 cup Italian-style salad dressing
235ml/1 cup mayonnaise
1 onion (chopped)
2 stalks celery (chopped)
1/2 tsp salt
Sprinkle of ground black pepper
Sprinkle of garlic powder

Method

1. Cook the pasta in a large pot of boiling salted water until al dente, and then drain.

2. Marinate the macaroni in Italian dressing for 2 to 3 hours, giving it a stir halfway through.

3. Mix the sour cream, mayonnaise, onion, celery, garlic powder, tuna, and salt and pepper into macaroni, and serve.

Pasta & Prawns Picchi Pacchi (Serves 2)

Ingredients

200g/2 cups spaghetti
300g/2 1/2 cups prawns
4 tbsps olive oil
1 tsp white wine
1 tsp salt
1 onion (finely chopped)
1 clove garlic (finely chopped)
200g/1 1/2 cups tomatoes (chopped)
small bunch parsley (chopped)

Method

1. Cook the pasta in a large pan of boiling salted water until al dente.

Pasta & Prawns Picchi Pacchi/cont.

2. Gently fry the onion and garlic in the olive oil, until the onion is soft but not coloured.

3. Add the tomatoes and cook for a few minutes before adding the prawns and the wine. Cook for a few minutes more, just long enough to heat the prawns through. Add the parsley.

4. Drain the pasta, toss with the sauce and serve.

Macaroni & Sardines (Serves 4)

Ingredients

6 salted anchovy fillets
375g/3 cups macaroni
400g/2 1/2 cups fresh sardines
1 large fennel bulb
1 tbsp salt
1 tbsp saffron powder
1 onion (peeled and finely chopped)
5 tbsps olive oil
5 tbsps raisins
2 tbsps pine kernels
Freshly ground black pepper

Method

1. Soak the anchovies for 1 hour then dry them on paper towels and remove any large bones. Remove the sardine heads and tails, and slit the sardines open along the underside. Clean them thoroughly, removing the back bones.

2. Trim and cut the fennel into quarters and cook both the bulb and the leaves in slightly salted water for about 15 minutes or until tender.

3. Remove the fennel and retain the cooking water. Once the fennel has cooled slightly roughly chop it. Heat the oil and fry the onion until golden. Add the anchovies and let them soften. Add the sardines and cook for another few minutes.

4. Stir in the fennel, raisins, pine kernels and saffron powder, or strained liquid from soaking the strands. Add salt and pepper to taste, and cook briefly to make a sauce.

5. Meanwhile, cook the pasta for 7 minutes or until al dente, and drain. Toss in the sauce, and then serve.

Monkfish Pasta with Lime Mayonnaise (Serves 2)

Ingredients

2 monkfish fillets (skinned and cubed)
170g/1 1/2 cups rigatoni
2.5cm piece fresh root ginger (peeled and finely chopped)
4 spring onions (finely chopped)
8 cherry tomatoes (quartered)
Rind and juice of 1 lime
150ml/2/3 cup white wine
1 jar of mayonnaise
150ml/2/3 cup double cream
115g/1 cup green beans
1 red apple (cored and sliced thinly)
2 tbsps flat leaf parsley (chopped roughly)
Paprika pepper (to garnish)

Method

1. Place the fish into a large pan and add the wine. Cover and simmer for 3-4 minutes. Allow to cool and set aside.

2. Cook the pasta according to the packet instructions, cool and set aside. To prepare the mayonnaise, mix together the ginger, lime,mayonnaise and double cream in a large bowl.

3. Gently stir in the remaining ingredients except the parsley. Garnish with ground black pepper, parsley and paprika.

33

Pasta & Mussels in White Wine Sauce (Serves 1)
Ingredients
200g/1 1/2 cups fresh mussels in shells (beards removed)
50ml/1/4 cup white wine
50ml/1/4 cup double cream
1 garlic clove (chopped)
1 shallot (sliced)
2 tbsps chopped fresh coriander
2 tbsps chopped fresh parsley
1 tbsp olive oil
150g/1 1/2 cups cooked pasta of your choice
Salt and freshly ground black pepper

Method

1. For the mussels, heat the olive oil in a lidded saucepan over a medium heat. Add the garlic and shallots and sauté for two minutes, until softened.

2. Add the mussels and white wine, stir well and place the lid on. Allow the mussels to steam for 3 minutes, then remove the lid and check that all the mussels are cooked and have opened. Discard any that have not opened.

3. Remove the mussels from their shells and return the flesh to the pan, discarding all of the shells. Add the double cream, fresh parsley and cooked pasta, stir together and season with salt and freshly ground black pepper.

4. To serve, place into a large bowl and sprinkle over the fresh coriander.

Prawn Penne (Serves 4)
Ingredients
255g/2 cups cooked peeled prawns
200g/2 cups penne pasta
1 garlic clove (chopped)
Bunch of fresh basil
1 lemon, juice only
2 tbsps olive oil
4 tbsps white wine
1 tbsp tomato purée

1 bay leaf

3 tbsps crème fraîche

1 tbsp plain flour

Parmesan shavings

Method

1. Cook the penne for 8 minutes in boiling salted water, strain and toss in olive oil. Preheat the olive oil in a pan and add the garlic, cooking until soft.

2. Add the flour and stir into the vegetables. Add the tomato purée, bay leaf, lemon juice, wine and reduce. Bring to the boil and reduce. Pass the liquid through a sieve and return to the pan. Add the cooked prawns and bring back to the boil and add the crème fraîche.

3. Add the cooked penne and then stir in half the parmesan and some torn basil leaves. Serve with a sprinkle of parmesan and some more basil.

Tuna Penne Salad (Serves 4)
Ingredients

150g/1 1/2 cups penne pasta (cooked until al dente)

150g/2 cups olives (chopped)

3 carrots (grated)

1 cucumber (seeds removed and grated)

2 tomatoes (chopped)

2 cans tuna (drained)

4 tbsps parmesan (grated)

2 tbsps olive oil

3 tbsps chopped fresh flatleaf parsley

Method

1. Place the grated carrot, cucumber and chopped tomatoes into a bowl and mix together.

2. Place the cooked penne into a large bowl with all the remaining ingredients (the heat from the pasta will heat the other ingredients to give you a warm pasta dish).

3. Serve both bowls of salad in one bowl together at the table.

Tuna Steak with Penne Pasta (Serves 1)
Ingredients
125g/1 cup penne pasta (cooked until al dente)
1/2 tomato (chopped)
1 fresh tuna steak
2 tbsps olive oil
Juice & zest of 1 lemon
Small handful of rocket lettuce
Salt and freshly ground black pepper

Method

1. Place the hot pasta, olive oil, lemon and rocket into a serving bowl, mixing the ingredients together.

2. Heat the extra oil in a frying pan on a high heat. Season the tuna, to taste, with salt and freshly ground black pepper on each side.

3. Place the tuna into the frying pan and fry for two minutes on each side, or until cooked to your liking. Remove the tuna from the frying pan and place on top of the pasta.

Sprinkle the chopped tomato over the top to serve.

Fresh Seafood Pasta (Serves 2)
Ingredients
150g mixed fresh seafood
150g linguine (cooked until al dente)
2 spring onions (chopped)
2 garlic cloves (chopped)
1 tbsp olive oil
1 tbsp butter
1 tbsp saffron powder
1 tbsp freshly grated parmesan

Method
1. Heat the olive oil and butter in a pan, add the spring onions and cook gently for 2-3 minutes.

2. Add the garlic and fry for another minute. Add the seafood and saffron, and cook for 2-3 minutes. Stir in the hot cooked pasta and mix well to coat.

3. To serve, place the seafood pasta into serving dishes and sprinkle with the grated parmesan.

Pasta with Prawn Sauce (Serves 1)

Ingredients

110g/1 cup prawns (cooked and peeled)
110g/1 cup spaghetti (cooked until al dente)
1 spring onion (finely chopped)
2 tbsps tomato sauce
1/2 garlic clove (crushed)
1 tbsp red wine vinegar
50ml/1/3 cup hot water
2 bell peppers (chopped)
1 tbsp tomato purée
2 tbsps olive oil
2 tbsps caster sugar
Salt and freshly ground black pepper

Method

1. Place all of the ingredients, except the prawns, basil and spaghetti, into a deep saucepan over a medium heat, season with salt and freshly ground black pepper and simmer for four minutes.

2. Transfer the tomato sauce to a food processor and blend until smooth. Return to the pan and simmer until the sauce reduces, about four minutes.

3. To serve, add the prawns and basil and stir through. Add the spaghetti and stir through again and transfer to a serving plate.

Prawn Linguine (Serves 4)

Ingredients

300g/2 1/2 cups raw peeled prawns
400g/3 cups dried linguine
500g/3 1/2 cups vine-ripened cherry tomatoes (halved)
2 tbsps olive oil
3 garlic cloves (finely chopped)
4 tsps fresh basil leaves (chopped)

Method

1. Preheat the oven to 200C/400F/Gas Mark 6. Spread the tomatoes over the base of a small roasting tin to fit tightly. Drizzle with 1 tablespoon olive oil and season. Roast for 25 minutes.

2. Meanwhile, run a small, sharp knife along the back of each prawn to just cut through the flesh. Pull away any small black veins that you find.

3. Bring a large pan of lightly salted water to the boil. Add the pasta and cook until al dente.

4. Just before the pasta is ready, heat the remaining oil in a large frying pan. Add the garlic, sizzle for a few seconds, then add the prawns. Toss them together over high heat for 2 minutes, until they are cooked through.

5. Drain the pasta, return it to the pan and add the roasted tomatoes, prawns, basil and some seasoning. Toss together well, divide between warmed pasta bowls and serve, scattered with a few small basil leaves.

Crayfish & Rocket Tagliatelle (Serves 4)

Ingredients

250g/2 cups tagliatelle pasta
300g/2 1/2 cups cooked crayfish tails
1/2 tsp saffron threads
2 tbsps olive oil
1 mild red chilli (chopped)
500g/3 1/2 cups halved cherry tomatoes
1 lemon
Rocket lettuce (to serve)

Method

1. Soak 1/2 tsp saffron threads in 2 tsps of boiling water for 30 minutes. Place the tagliatelle into a pan, along with the saffron water, and boil for 2-3 minutes, and drain.

2. Heat the olive oil in a pan. Add the chilli and tomatoes, and cook for 3 minutes. Stir in the juice of 1 lemon and the crayfish tails, until hot.

3. Toss with the pasta and serve with rocket lettuce.

Tuna & Lemon Spaghetti (Serves 2)
Ingredients
250g/2 cups spaghetti
1 tuna steak
Juice of 1 small lemon
9 tbsps extra-virgin olive oil
2 shallots (finely chopped)
1 garlic clove (very thinly sliced)
1 long red chilli (deseeded and finely chopped)
Large handful fresh flat leaf parsley (chopped)

Method

1. Bring a large pan of salted water to the boil. Add the spaghetti and cook according to packet instructions. Drain, then return to the pan.

2. Meanwhile, make the sauce. Heat 4 tablespoons of the oil in a frying pan over a medium heat, add the shallots and garlic and cook for 2 minutes. Add the chilli and cook for a further 2 minutes, until everything is softened.

3. Add the tuna, lemon juice and parsley and mix together. Add the remaining oil (this will act as a dressing for the pasta), and stir over the heat for 1 minute to heat through.

4. Cut the cooked tuna steak into strips, toss through the cooked spaghetti and season to taste.

5. Divide between 2 warm bowls and serve.

Shrimp-ed Spaghetti (Serves 2-4)

Ingredients

900g/6 cups shrimp (deveined)
450g/3 cups whole wheat spaghetti
450g/2 cups of canned chopped tomatoes (in puree)
2 cloves of garlic (crushed)
225g/1 cup of onion (finely chopped)
225g tomato puree
2 tbsps fresh basil (chopped)
2 tsps olive oil
1 tsp oregano

Method

1. Cook the spaghetti as per the packet instructions, (time in with the end of cooking the shrimp).

2. Whilst the spaghetti is cooking, place the olive oil in a large non-stick frying pan and place over a medium heat.

3. Add in the onion and garlic and fry for 3-4 minutes, until softened.

4. Add in the tomato puree and chopped tomatoes and sprinkle in some oregano. Simmer gently for 10-15 minutes, until the sauce begins to reduce and thicken. Stir in the shrimp and heat well for 5-6 minutes.

5. Drain the pasta and add the sauce and shrimps, toss well. Serve and sprinkle with the chopped basil.

Grilled Cajun Red Snapper & Pasta (Serves 4)

Ingredients

300g/2 cups tagliatelle pasta
550g/3 cups red snapper fillets (divided into 4)
2 tsps olive oil
2 tbsps Cajun seasoning
Juice of 1 lime
Juice of 1 lemon

Method

1. Place the lemon juice, lime juice, olive oil and Cajun seasoning in a bowl, (large enough to take the fillets) and mix together well. Meanwhile, cook the pasta until al dente.

2. Place the red snapper fillets in the bowl and cover well with the dressing. Cover and place in the refrigerator to marinate for 30 minutes.

3. Heat the grill to a medium setting and spray the grill pan with low-fat cooking spray.

4. Lay the fillets on the grill pan and place under the grill for 6-8 minutes, (depending on the thickness of the fillets).

Season with pepper and herbs if desired.

Cajun Seafood Pasta (Serves 6)

Ingredients

100g/1 cup chopped green onions
455g/3 1/2 cups dry fettuccine pasta
60g/1/2 cup chopped parsley
225g/2 cups shrimp, peeled and deveined
225g/1 3/4 cups scallops
475ml/2 cups whipping cream
2 tsps salt
3 tbsps shredded Swiss cheese
3 tbsps grated Parmesan cheese
1 tsp chopped fresh basil
1 tsp chopped fresh thyme
1 tsp ground black pepper
1 tsp crushed red pepper flakes

Method

1. Cook pasta in a large pot of boiling salted water until al dente. Meanwhile, pour cream into large skillet. Cook over medium heat, stirring constantly, until just about boiling.

Cajun Seafood Pasta/cont.

2. Reduce heat, and add herbs, salt, pepper, onions, and parsley. Simmer for 7 to 8 minutes, or until thickened.

3. Stir in seafood, cooking until shrimps are no longer transparent. Stir in cheeses, blending well.

Drain pasta and serve together.

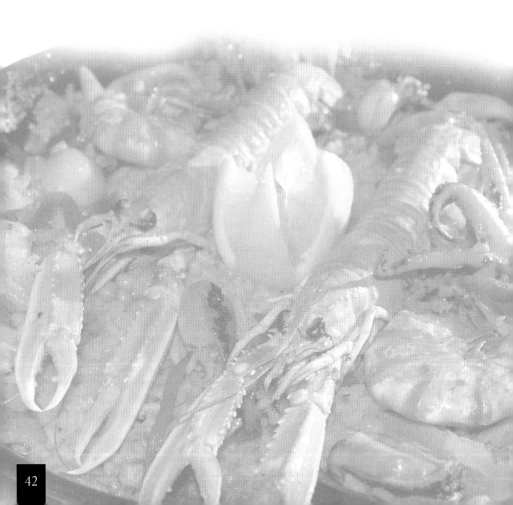

One-Pot Macaroni & Cheese (Serves 2)

Ingredients

710ml/3 cups water ✕
225g/1 cup seashell pasta ✕
235ml/1 cup whole fat milk ✕
450g/2 1/4 cups shredded Cheddar cheese ✕
80g/1/2 cup shredded Parmesan cheese ✕
1 tsp salt ✕
1 tsp Dijon mustard (optional) ✕
Sprinkle of ground black pepper ✕

Method

1. Pour the water and salt into a medium sized pot and bring to a boil over a high heat. Once the water is boiling, stir in the shell pasta, and return to a boil.

2. Cook the pasta uncovered, stirring occasionally, until the water has cooked down a bit, for about 5 minutes. Stir in the milk, and continue boiling for another 5 minutes.

3. Add the Cheddar, Parmesan, pepper, and mustard, and stir until the cheese melts and the sauce is thick and creamy. The starch from the pasta thickens the sauce as the pasta cooks.

Tomato and Basil Sauce (Serves 6)
Ingredients

1 large onion, chopped
3 cans of chopped tomatoes
2 garlic cloves, crushed
1 large handful basil leaves (torn into small pieces)
3 tbsps olive oil
2 tsps balsamic vinegar
2 tsps sugar
1/2 tsp dried chilli flakes
Sprinkle of salt
Sprinkle of freshly ground black pepper
Grated parmesan cheese (optional)

Method

1. Heat the olive oil in a large frying pan and cook the onion and garlic until slightly softened. Stir in the tomatoes, chilli flakes, sugar and balsamic vinegar.

2. Bring to a simmer and cook slowly for 1 hour. Stir in the basil and season with salt and pepper. Blend in a food processor for a smooth sauce, or just leave it for a chunkier sauce.

3. Serve spooned over cooked pasta with plenty of parmesan cheese.

Golden Lasagne (Serves 4)
Ingredients

6 lasagne sheets
40g/1/4 cup chopped onion
175g/1 cup sliced mushrooms
45ml/1/3 cup chicken broth
1 tin of cream of chicken soup
80ml/1/3 cup milk
1/2 tsp dried basil
450g/2 cups diced chicken breast meat
455g/3 cups ricotta cheese
170g/1 1/3 cup shredded Cheddar cheese
2 tsps grated Parmesan cheese

Method

1. Preheat oven to 350F/180C/Gas Mark 4. Fill 3/4 of a large pot with lightly salted water and bring to a boil. Add lasagne sheets and cook for 8 to 10 minutes or until al dente, and then drain.

2. In a small saucepan, saute the onion and mushrooms in the chicken broth. Remove from heat, then stir in soup, milk and basil, stirring well for 2 minutes. Set aside for now.

3. In a lightly greased baking dish, arrange 3 cooked lasagne sheets. Then add the following layers in this exact order - 1/2 the chicken, 1/2 the ricotta cheese, 1/2 the Cheddar cheese, 1/2 the Parmesan cheese and 1/2 the mushroom/soup mixture. Add the other 3 lasagne sheets and repeat layers.

4. Bake uncovered in the preheated oven for approximately 50 minutes. Allow to cool for a few minutes before serving.

Bolognese Sauce

Ingredients

225g/1 1/4 cups minced beef
4 smoked bacon rashers
1 green pepper (seeded and diced)
2 cans tinned tomatoes
1 clove garlic (peeled and crushed)
1 onion (peeled and finely chopped)
1 carrot (peeled and diced)
150ml/2/3 cup red wine
2 tbsps olive oil
1 tbsp mixed dried herbs

Method

1. Heat a frying pan and add half of the mince. Cook over a high heat to colour the meat, breaking up any lumps with a fork. Repeat with the rest of the mince and drain off any fat.

2. Heat the oil in another large pan and cook the onion, carrot and green pepper until they start to soften.

Bolognaise Sauce/cont.

3. Stir in the garlic, bacon and herbs, and cook for 2 minutes. Add in the tomatoes and the wine and season well.

4. Add the mince and simmer gently for 40-50 minutes until thick. Best served with spaghetti.

Spaghetti Carbonara (Serves 2)

Ingredients

4 smoked bacon rashers
1 garlic clove (finely chopped)
300g/2 cups dried spaghetti
3 small eggs
140ml/2/3 cup single cream
5 tbsps parmesan cheese (grated)
1 tbsp olive oil
Green salad (to serve)

Method

1. Fry the bacon and garlic in olive oil in a pan until crisp. Set to one side and leave to cool.

2. Cook the spaghetti according to the packet instructions, until al dente. In a side bowl, mix the eggs, single cream and two tablespoons of grated parmesan.

3. Once combined, add the cooked bacon. Drain the spaghetti, return to the pan and immediately pour in the carbonara sauce.

4. Toss well to coat and allow the egg to 'set' slightly.

Serve with a green salad and the remaining parmesan sprinkled on top.

Vegetable Bolognese (Serves 4)

Ingredients

1 tbsp olive oil
250g/2 cups dried spaghetti
1 red onion, chopped
1 large garlic clove, crushed
3 carrots (finely sliced)
1 red pepper (deseeded and chopped)
75g/3 oz mushrooms (chopped)
500g/4 cups creamed tomatoes
50g/1/3 cup broccoli, chopped
Handful of fresh basil leaves

Method

1. Heat the oil in a large pan, add the onion and garlic and fry for a few minutes to soften but not colour.

2. Add the carrots and cook for 5 minutes, then add the pepper and cook for a further 2 minutes.

3. Stir in the mushrooms and creamed tomatoes and bring to the boil. Add the broccoli and basil leaves and simmer for 5 minutes or until all the vegetables are tender.

4. Whisk the vegetables in a food processor, in batches, until very finely sliced and chopped. Return the sauce to a saucepan to warm it through completely.

5. Meanwhile, bring a large saucepan of water to the boil and cook the spaghetti according to packet instructions.

Drain and toss through the sauce to serve.

Vegetable Lasagne (Serves 4-6)

Ingredients

4 dried lasagne sheets
1 butternut squash (chopped)
1 courgette (chopped)
1 carrot (diced)
225g/1 cup of mushrooms (sliced)
1 celery stalk (chopped)
1 onion (finely chopped)
1 clove of garlic (crushed)
900g/4 cups of canned chopped tomatoes
2 tbsps tomato puree
1 tsp oregano
1 tsp mixed herbs
225g/1 cup of spinach (chopped)
2 tsps olive oil
450g/2 cups of low-fat ricotta cheese (or quark)
170g/3/4 cup of low-fat mozzarella cheese

Method

1. Preheat the oven to 190/375F/Gas mark 5. Spray a 11 x 7 inch baking dish with low-fat cooking spray.

2. Place the olive oil in a large saucepan and place over a medium heat. Add the garlic and onion and sauté for 2-3 minutes. Add the celery, mushrooms, carrots, courgettes and squash and gently sauté for approximately 10 minutes, until the vegetables have softened.

3. Add in the tomato puree, chopped tomatoes, herbs and black pepper. Bring to the boil, reduce the heat and simmer for 10 minutes. Stir in the spinach.

4. Spoon a cup of the sauce on the base of the baking dish. Top with a layer of lasagne sheets, followed by a layer of ricotta cheese, (or quark). Add another layer of sauce, followed by lasagne sheets and ricotta cheese.

5. Continue this process and end with a layer of sauce. Top with the mozzarella cheese. Place in the oven and bake for 30 minutes.

Marinara Linguine (Serves 6)

Ingredients

900g/5 cups fresh linguine

14 tomatoes (cut into 1-inch chunks)

4 cloves of garlic (crushed)

4 tbsps tomato puree

3 tbsps olive oil

1 tbsp fresh basil

1 tbsp oregano (finely chopped)

3/4 tsp salt

2 sweet onions (finely chopped)**

Grated mozzarella

** Sweet onions are available in the UK between July and September.

Method

1. Add 1 tbsp olive oil to a pan and heat. Add in the onions and sauté for 3-5 minutes, until tender. Add the crushed garlic and cook, stirring continuously for 30 seconds.

2. Add in the tomato puree and tomatoes and stir in well. Bring to the boil and simmer for 15 minutes, stirring intermittently.

3. Towards the end of the 15 minutes, cook the linguine as per the packet instructions, (3-4 minutes if fresh). Drain and place on a large serving dish.

4. Remove the tomato sauce from the heat and stir in the fresh basil, oregano and 2 tbsp olive oil. Pour over the linguine and serve.

Sprinkle with mozzarella.

Pesto Sauce (Serves 2)

Ingredients

150g/1 1/2 cups fresh basil leaves
350ml/1 1/2 cups olive oil
3 cloves of garlic (roughly diced)
2 tbsps pine nuts
1 tsp salt
175g/1 1/2 cups freshly grated Parmesan cheese
2 tbsps butter

Method

1. Using a blender, put in the basil and garlic and mix for a few seconds. Then add the pine nuts and olive oil and salt, and blend at a high speed until the sauce approaches being creamy.

2. When the blending is completed, transfer the sauce into a mixing bowl and stir in the grated cheese, and then the softened butter, making sure you get a good creamy sauce. It is now ready for combining with your favourite pasta!

Gorgonzola Sauce (Serves 2)

Ingredients

1/4 lb fresh gorgonzola
75ml/1/3 cup milk
3 tbsps of butter
120ml/1/2 cup whipping cream
Salt and pepper
50g/1/4 cup freshly grated parmesan

Method

1. In a sauté pan, over medium-low heat, put in the milk and the butter, plus 1/2 teaspoon of salt and a few grounds of pepper. As the milk comes almost to a boil, reduce the heat to low, add the gorgonzola and stir for a few minutes to obtain a cream-like texture.

2. Now add the whipping cream to the sauce, and over medium heat, reduce it slightly. Take off the heat and await the pasta. Remember to re-heat the sauce for at least a minute just before the pasta is ready.

Lamb Ragu Sauce (Serves 2)

Ingredients

55ml/1/4 cup olive oil
2 garlic cloves (peeled and minced)
1 tsp chopped rosemary
1 bay leaf
2 tbsps finely diced onion
250g/1 1/2 cups lamb mince
120ml/1/2 cup white wine
4 tomatoes (chopped)
200g/1 cup meat stock
1 tbsp fresh parsley (chopped)
Salt and pepper

Method

1. Heat the olive oil in a deep saucepan over medium heat. Add garlic and the onion and cook until the onion is slightly tender, about three minutes. Add the rosemary and the bay leaf and cook for another minute.

2. Increase the heat to medium high and add the lamb. Saute and stir until the lamb is browned, about five minutes. Add the wine and scrape up the bottom of the pan.

3. Add the tomatoes, the stock and a teaspoon of salt. Simmer until the lamb is tender, about 1 1/2 hours. Watch the liquidity of the sauce: add more stock or water if the sauce is getting too thick.

Taste for salt and pepper and serve with gnocchi or any of your favourite pastas.

Basic Tomato Sauce (Serves 4)

Ingredients

24 tomatoes
70ml/1/3 cup olive oil
5 cloves of garlic
60g/1/2 cup basil (torn by hand)
1 tsp salt
1 tsp sugar

Basic Tomato Sauce/cont.
Method
1. Wash the tomatoes. Cut them in half, then again, into quarters. Put the oil and garlic into a saucepan over medium heat.

2. As soon as you hear the garlic start to sizzle, immediately put in the tomatoes, add the salt and cook, uncovered over a low/medium heat, for about 10 minutes.

3. About two minutes before the tomatoes are finished cooking (at about 8 minutes) add the basil, stir a few times, and serve with pasta.

Puttanesca Sauce (Serves 4)
Ingredients
55ml/1/4 cup olive oil
6 anchovy fillets (chopped)
4 garlic cloves (minced)
450g/4 cups linguine
2 large cans peeled Italian plum tomatoes
2 tsps fresh oregano (chopped)
60g/1/2 cup black olives
3 tbsps capers
55g/1/2 cup parsley (chopped)
Pinch of red pepper flakes
Salt to taste

Method
1. Cook the linguine until tender but still firm. Drain, and transfer to heated plates. Drain the tomatoes and cut them into halves, and squeeze out as much liquid as possible.

2. Heat olive oil slightly over medium heat in a large skillet. Put in anchovy and cook, stirring, to break up anchovy. Add garlic and cook for 1 minute, to release the flavour. Do not allow garlic to burn. Stir in tomatoes and bring to a boil.

3. Lower the heat and keep sauce at a rolling, strong simmer. Add the remaining ingredients (except pasta) one at a time, stirring frequently. Taste for seasoning and add salt if necessary. Remember that anchovy is salty.

4. Reduce heat to a low simmer and continue to cook for a few minutes, or until sauce has thickened to your own taste. When sauce is close to finished, cook the pasta until al dente. Drain, and transfer to heated plates. Coat the pasta with the sauce and top with parsley.

Pepperoni Pasta (Serves 4)
Ingredients
450g ground beef
1 medium onion (chopped)
1 medium green pepper (chopped)
1 garlic clove (minced)
1 jar (28 oz) spaghetti sauce
1 can (4 oz) mushroom pieces (drained)
1 packet sliced pepperoni
200g/1 1/2 cups penne pasta
150g/1 cup shredded mozzarella cheese
4 ounces provolone cheese (shredded)
Grated Parmesan cheese

Method

1. In a large skillet, cook the beef, onion, green pepper and garlic over medium heat until the meat is no longer pink, then drain. Add spaghetti sauce, mushrooms and pepperoni.

2. In a greased baking dish (approximately 14 inches x 10 inches), layer half of the pasta and beef mixture. Sprinkle with 1/2 cup each mozzarella and provolone.

3. Repeat layers until it is all used up, then sprinkle with Parmesan cheese. Bake, uncovered, at 200C/400F/Gas Mark 6 for 30-35 minutes or until heated through.

Serve with grated Parmesan cheese.

Vegetable Fettuccine (Serves 4)

Ingredients

4 sliced carrots

1 sliced courgette

2 broccoli florets

150g/5 oz green beans, halved

300g/3 cups fettuccine

200g/1 1/3 cups low-fat cottage cheese

150m/2/3 cup skimmed milk

2 tsps basil

50g/1/4 cup chopped parsley

Method

1. Steam carrots, courgette, broccoli, and green beans until tender. Put in a serving bowl to cool. Cook pasta according to package directions, drain and set aside to cool.

2. Using a blender or a food processor, puree cottage cheese until smooth. Blend in skimmed milk, basil, and parsley. Combine vegetables and pasta.

3. Pour sauce over cool vegetables and pasta and mix until they are thoroughly coated. Serve at room temperature.

Spring Vegetables & Spaghetti (Serves 2)

Ingredients

225g/8 oz dried spaghetti
400g/2 cups mixed spring vegetables (carrots, spring onions etc) (chopped)
1 small onion (finely chopped)
225ml/1 cup single cream
1 garlic clove (finely chopped)
Zest of 1 lemon
110ml/1/2 cup dry white wine
Small bunch mixed herbs (finely chopped)
2 tsps extra virgin olive oil
Parmesan shavings (to serve)

Method

1. Bring a pan of lightly salted water to a boil. Blanch the vegetables for 2 minutes.

2. Drain and use the water to cook the pasta. Cook the pasta until tender. Drain the pasta and set to one side. Cook the onion and garlic in a pan with a little oil until soft, but not coloured.

3. Add the drained vegetables and cook for a couple of minutes. Add the wine to the mix, bring to the boil and reduce by about half.

4. Next, add the cream and lemon zest and bring back to the boil. Add the pasta, stirring well and allow to cook through.

5. Add the herbs, season and stir well before serving topped with shavings of parmesan.

Sprinkle with black pepper.

Creamy Mushroom Ravioli (Serves 4)

Ingredients

400g/14 oz brown mushrooms (thinly sliced)
400g/14 oz ravioli
2 garlic cloves (peeled and thinly sliced)
500ml/2 cups milk
6 sprigs fresh thyme, leaves picked
3 tsps cornflour
2 tsps olive oil
1 egg, lightly whisked
Salt & freshly ground black pepper
6 green shallots, ends trimmed, thinly sliced diagonally

Method

1. Heat the olive oil in a large frying pan over a medium heat. Add the garlic, mushroom and thyme, and cook, stirring every now and again until mushrooms are tender.

2. Combine cornflour and a little of the milk in a medium bowl. Gradually whisk in the remaining milk and egg until well combined, and season with salt and pepper.

3. Add the milk mixture to the mushroom mixture and stir over a medium heat for 5 minutes or until the mixture begins to thicken slightly. Stir well once complete.

4. Meanwhile, cook the ravioli in salted boiling water until al dente. Drain well, and return to the pan.

5. Add two-thirds of the green shallot to the mushroom mixture and stir until combined. Add mushroom mixture to the ravioli and gently toss until just combined.

6. Spoon ravioli among serving bowls. Sprinkle with the remaining shallots and serve immediately.

Wild Mushroom Tagliatelle (Serves 4)

Ingredients

300g/11 oz chestnuts
50g/1/3 cup butter
2 shallots (finely chopped)
200g/2 cups wild mushrooms, cleaned
50ml/1/4 cup brandy
175ml/3/4 cup double cream
500g/4 cups fresh tagliatelle pasta
2 tbsps flat leaf parsley (finely chopped)
2 tbsps chervil (finely chopped)
2 tbsps parmesan (freshly grated)

Method

1. Preheat the oven to 220C/425F/Gas Mark 7. Pierce each chestnut with a knife, making a small slit in the shell - this prevents them from exploding in the oven. Place the chestnuts onto a baking tray and roast in the oven for 20-25 minutes, until tender.

2. Remove from the oven and allow to cool, then peel, and roughly chop. Heat a frying pan until hot, add the butter and shallots and cook for 1-2 minutes.

3. Add the mushrooms and fry for a further one minute. Add the brandy and carefully set light to the brandy with a match or by tilting the pan towards the flame.

4. Add the cream and chestnuts and bring to the boil. Reduce the heat and simmer for two minutes. Meanwhile, bring a large pan of salted water to the boil, add the pasta and cook until al dente. Drain the pasta, then add to the sauce.

5. Add the parsley, chervil and parmesan and season, to taste, with salt and freshly ground black pepper. Mix well and serve in bowls.

Mushroom Cannelloni (Serves 4)

Ingredients

2 tbsps butter
550g/4 cups shitake mushrooms (chopped)
100ml/1/2 cup double cream
150g/2 cups spinach (chopped)
200g/1 1/2 cups ricotta (drained)
1 tsp freshly grated nutmeg
4 large sheets fresh pasta
250g/2 cups Roquefort cheese (crumbled)
1 free-range egg yolk
1 tbsp chopped fresh mint
Salt and freshly ground black pepper
Chopped fresh tomatoes and olive oil (to serve)

Method

1. Heat the butter in a pan and fry the mushrooms until soft. Season well with salt and freshly ground black pepper. Stir in the spinach and mint until wilted, then drain off any excess liquid.

2. In a bowl, beat the ricotta with the nutmeg and season well with salt and freshly ground black pepper. Add the mushroom mixture to the bowl and mix well.

3. Lay the blanched pasta sheets on a clean work surface and place some of the filling mixture along one edge of each sheet. Roll up into a cigar shape and place seal-side down into a greased ovenproof dish.

4. For the topping, beat the Roquefort and egg yolk together in a bowl until smooth, then add the cream and stir to combine. Chill in the fridge for 30 minutes until set.

5. Preheat the oven to 180C/350F/Gas Mark 4. Spread the topping mixture over the cannelloni. Cover the dish with aluminium foil and bake in the oven for 8-10 minutes, until warmed through.

6. Preheat the grill to medium. Remove the aluminium foil and place the cannelloni under the grill for 2-3 minutes, until golden-brown and bubbling.

7. To serve, sprinkle the cannelloni with chopped tomatoes and a drizzle of olive oil.

Chocolate & Orange Pasta Pancakes (Serves 2-4)

Ingredients

4 free-range eggs
1 orange, finely grated zest only
2 tbsp cocoa powder
1 tbsp icing sugar
25g/1oz butter
85g/3/4 cup fettucine pasta (cooked until al dente)

Method

1. Preheat the oven to 220C/425F/Gas Mark 7. Whisk the eggs and orange zest together in a large bowl.

2. Sift in the cocoa powder and icing sugar and whisk again to combine.

3. Heat the butter in a heavy-based ovenproof frying pan and add the cooked pasta. Pour in the egg mixture.

4. Transfer to the oven for 4-5 minutes until the eggs are just set.
Serve immediately.

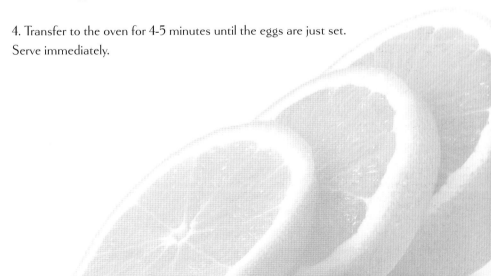

Dolcelatte & Broccoli Pasta (Serves 1)

Ingredients

100g/1 cup broccoli, cut into florets
150g/1 1/2 cups penne pasta (cooked until al dente)
75ml/1/3 cup double cream
75g/1/2 cup dolcelatte cheese

Method

1. Place the broccoli into boiling water and cook for four minutes or until just tender. Remove with a slotted spoon and place into a large bowl.

2. Add the cooked pasta, cream and cheese and stir until the cheese has melted into the cream sauce.

3. Transfer to a clean warm bowl and serve immediately.

Mediterranean Pasta Salad (Serves 2-3)

Ingredients

340g/3 cups pasta shapes (cooked and drained)
1 large aubergine (sliced thickly)
2-3 red onions (peeled and cut into wedges)
3 courgettes (halved lengthways)
1 red and 1 yellow pepper (de-seeded and cut into quarters)
1 tbsp olive oil
Sea salt and cracked black pepper
1 tbsp balsamic vinegar
2 tsps parmesan

Method

1. Preheat the grill to a medium heat. Toss the vegetables in olive oil and season with salt and pepper. Grill the peppers first. Cook skin side down until the skin becomes charred. Remove, peel off the skin, cut into strips and set aside.

2. Grill the remaining vegetables until soft and crisping at the edges. Remove and cut the aubergine and courgettes into chunks.

3. Stir the vegetables through the cooked pasta and add balsamic vinegar. Serve topped with parmesan shavings.

Halloumi and Tomato Pasta (Serves 1)

Ingredients

2 tbsps olive oil
1/2 red onion, finely chopped
1 clove garlic, chopped
pinch dried chilli flakes
100g/1 cup halloumi (chopped)
2 tomatoes (seeds removed and finely chopped)
150g/1 cup penne pasta (cooked until al dente)
2 tbsps chopped fresh basil

Method

1. Heat the olive oil in a frying pan over a medium heat. Add the onion, garlic and chilli flakes and fry for 2-3 minutes, until softened. Add the halloumi and fry for 2-3 minutes, until golden.

2. Add the finely chopped tomato, pasta and basil and stir together and warm through. To serve, place into a warm bowl and season, to taste, with salt and freshly ground black pepper.

Feta Pasta (Serves 2)

Ingredients

2 tbsps pine nuts
100g/1 cup fine green beans, trimmed
250g/2 cups conchiglie pasta
100g/3/4 cup baby spinach leaves
150g/1 1/2 cups cherry tomatoes (halved)
3 tbsps olive oil
100g/1/2 cup feta cheese
Small handful fresh basil leaves

Method

1. In a large saucepan, fry the pine nuts for 1-2 minutes, until golden. Remove and set aside. Using the same pan, fill with cold water and bring to the boil.

2. Add the beans and blanch for 2 minutes. Remove with a slotted spoon, and refresh under cold running water – this will help them keep their bright green colour. Set aside.

Feta Pasta/cont.

3. Add the pasta and a pinch of salt to the boiling water and cook according to packet instructions. Drain and briefly run under cold running water to cool slightly, then return to the pan.

4. Put the spinach leaves in a colander and pour over a kettle of boiling water to wilt them. Refresh under cold running water, then squeeze out as much excess water as you can.

5. Toss the spinach through the pasta, then add the beans, tomatoes and dressing. Season. Divide between 2 bowls. Sprinkle with toasted nuts and crumble over the feta.

Scatter with basil leaves to serve.

Cauliflower Pasta (Serves 4)
Ingredients

2 tbsps olive oil
200g/1 cup mushrooms, thickly sliced
500g/3 1/2 cups dried spaghetti
1 onion (sliced)
1 red pepper (deseeded and sliced)
1 large garlic clove (crushed)
1 courgette (halved lengthways then sliced)
400g/2 1/2 cups cherry tomatoes in tomato juice, or chopped tomatoes
4 tbsps green pesto
Parmesan shavings (optional)

Method

1. Put a large saucepan of water on to boil for the pasta. Meanwhile, heat the oil in a large frying pan over a medium heat. Add the onion and pepper and cook, stirring, for 5 minutes.

2. Add the garlic and courgette, cook for 5 minutes, then add the tomatoes. Half-fill the can with water then pour into the pan.

3. Add the mushrooms. Bring to the boil, then reduce the heat and simmer for 5 minutes. Season to taste.

4. While the sauce is cooking, cook the spaghetti according to packet instructions or until al dente. Drain and return to the pan.

5. Stir the pesto into the spaghetti and divide between 4 bowls. Top with the sauce and Parmesan shavings, if desired. Serve with garlic bread.

Pasta & Couscous Salad (Serves 2)

Ingredients

450g/2 cups of cooked whole wheat couscous
225g/1 cup of canned chickpeas (drained)
200g/1 1/2 cups penne pasta
Juice of 2 lemons
225g/1 cup of cucumber (chopped)
1/2 red onion (finely chopped)
225g/1 cup of tomatoes (chopped)
1 tbsp olive oil
1/3 cup of fresh mint

Method

1. To make the dressing, place the lemon juice and olive oil in a bowl and whisk together.

2. In a separate bowl place the couscous, tomato, onion, chickpeas, cucumber and mint.

3. Pour the dressing over the salad and gently toss, coating all the ingredients.

Cover and place in the refrigerator for 2-3 hours.

Red Pepper Pasta (Serves 4)
Ingredients
900g/4 cups of roasted red sweet peppers (drained)
225g/8 oz penne pasta
3 cloves garlic (crushed)
1 piece of fresh basil
2 tsps virgin olive oil
225ml/1 cup of water
110g/1/2 cup of tomato puree
2 tbsps red wine vinegar
Fresh grated Parmesan cheese (optional)

Method
1. Heat the olive oil in a frying pan and heat over a medium/high heat and sauté the onions until golden brown.

2. Place half the crushed garlic and half of the red peppers in a food processor and blend until the mixture is almost smooth.

3. Add in half of the basil, tomato puree, water and red wine vinegar and blend until the mixture is almost smooth. Pour the mixture into a saucepan.

4. Add the remaining garlic, basil, peppers, tomato puree, water and red wine vinegar to the blender and process, as before. Pour into the saucepan with the other sauce mixture.

5. Cook over a medium heat for 10 minutes, whilst cooking the pasta in another saucepan, (cook as per packet instructions).

6. Drain the pasta and remove the sauce from the heat. Pour over the pasta and serve.

Sprinkle over with fresh Parmesan cheese, if desired.

Crunchy-Vegetable Spaghetti (Serves 4)

Ingredients for Spaghetti:

300g/11 oz of spaghetti

2 carrots (peeled & sliced julienne)

2 medium leeks (trimmed & finely shredded)

225g/1 cup of celeriac (peeled & sliced julienne)

1 red pepper (deseeded & sliced)

1 yellow pepper (deseeded & sliced)

2 cloves of garlic (crushed)

1 tsp celery seeds

1 tbsp lemon juice

Ingredients for Lemon Dressing:

1 tbsp lemon juice

1 tsp finely grated lemon rind

2 tbsps snipped chives

4 tbsps low-fat fromage frais

Salt & pepper (to season)

Method

1. Place all of the vegetables in a large bowl and add the celery seeds and lemon juice. Toss well, coating all the vegetables well.

2. Cook the spaghetti, as per the packet instructions. Drain and mix in a little olive oil, (to stop it sticking together). Keep warm.

3. Whilst the spaghetti is cooking, place the vegetables in a steamer or sieve and place over a pan of boiling water.

4. Cover and steam for 5-7 minutes, or until the vegetables are just tender. Place the lemon dressing ingredients in a bowl and mix together well.

5. Transfer the spaghetti and vegetables into a warmed serving bowl and mix together well with the dressing. Serve immediately.

Tortellini with Pumpkin, Sage and Cheese Sauce (Serves 4)

Ingredients

1 butternut pumpkin approximately 1kg (peeled, deseeded, chopped)
2 tbsps sage leaves (roughly chopped)
1 garlic clove (crushed)
1 tbsp olive oil
500g packet tortellini pasta
220ml/1 cup single cream
40g/1/3 cup grated parmesan cheese
Small sage leaves (to serve)

Method

1. Preheat oven to 220C/450F/Gas Mark 7. Place pumpkin, sage, garlic, oil, and salt and pepper into a large roasting pan. Toss well to combine. Roast for 20 minutes or until pumpkin is tender.

2. Cook pasta in a saucepan of boiling salted water, following packet directions, until al dente, and drain.

3. Combine pumpkin mixture, cream, parmesan, pasta, and salt and pepper in a baking dish. Bake for 15 minutes or until bubbling and golden. Sprinkle with extra sage leaves and serve.

Stuffed Pasta Shells (Serves 4)
Ingredients
450g/4 cups large pasta shells

275g/2 cups ricotta cheese

60g/1/3 cup Parmesan cheese, grated

150g/1 cup mozzarella cheese, (grated)

4 tbsps fresh parsley (chopped)

1 tsp nutmeg

900ml/4 cups Italian tomato sauce

Method
1. Preheat the oven to 180C/350F/Gas Mark 4. Boil the pasta shells until done, drain, and set aside.

2. Meanwhile, combine cheeses, parsley, and nutmeg. Spoon enough tomato sauce into the baking dish to cover the bottom.

3. Fill shells and place in a single layer in the pan. Top with remaining sauce, cover with foil, and bake for 30 minutes, then serve.

Kosherie (Serves 4)
Ingredients
100g/3/4 cup lentils

200g/1 cup basmati rice

200g/1 1/2 cups elbow macaroni

3 tsps salt

12 tomatoes (chopped)

2 cloves garlic (minced)

1 fresh green chilli (chopped)

3 tbsps vegetable oil

1 tbsp red wine vinegar

6 small onions (thinly sliced)

Method
1. Combine lentils with water, and 1/2 tsp of salt in saucepan and bring to a boil. Reduce heat, cover, and simmer, stirring occasionally, about 40 minutes, until tender. If there's any water left, drain it before setting the lentils aside.

Kosherie/cont.

2. Meanwhile, place tomatoes, garlic, chilli, 1 tbsp vegetable oil, vinegar, and 1 tsp of salt in blender and purée. Pour into another saucepan over high heat and boil, then reduce heat and simmer with no lid for 25 minutes, stirring occasionally.

3. Rinse the rice and drain. Heat the rest of the oil in a third saucepan, add rice, some water, and 1/2 tsp salt, cover, and bring to a boil. Reduce to very low heat and simmer about 15 minutes, until rice is cooked and water is gone.

4. Meanwhile, add half the onions to a pan and fry them, stirring frequently, for about 10 minutes, until brown. Place on paper towels to drain, and sprinkle with a dash of salt. Repeat with the other onions.

5. When the hot sauce is ready, set aside and bring a pot of water to boil for the macaroni. Cook until al dente and drain.

Serve all together, with the rice on the side.

Gnocchi and Leek Soup

Ingredients

2 tbsps butter
375g/3 cups leeks, sliced
1 stick celery, finely sliced
375g/3 cups gnocchi
900ml/4 cups vegetable stock
142ml/2/3 cup carton single cream

Method

1. Melt the butter in a large pan and cook the leeks until softened but not coloured.

2. Add the celery, pasta, stock and seasoning. Bring to the boil, then cover and simmer for 20 minutes. Puree the soup in a blender and return to the rinsed pan. Heat through, then stir in the cream and serve.

Spicy Marrow & Pasta Soup

Ingredients

25g/1 oz butter
1 small onion, finely chopped
1 garlic clove, crushed
1 tbsp smoked paprika
1 tbsp tomato puree
1 marrow peeled, deseeded and cut into 2cm dice
1 vegetable stock cube made up with 600ml boiling water
400ml/1 3/4 cups coconut milk

Method

1. Heat the oil and butter in a large saucepan, then add the onions and cook over a moderate heat for 3-4 minutes or until softened. Then add the garlic, paprika and tomato puree and cook for a further minute. Add the marrow and stock and bring to the boil, then simmer for 10-12 minutes or until the marrow is tender to the point of a knife.

2. Transfer to a liquidiser and process until smooth. Return to the rinsed saucepan, then add the coconut milk and gently heat through. Season accordingly. Serve with chunks of crusty bread.

Spicy Beetroot, Coconut and Penne Soup

Ingredients for soup

500g/1.1lbs raw beetroots
2 tbsps vegetable oil
2 banana shallots, finely chopped
1 tsp cumin seeds
150g/5 oz penne pasta
600ml/2 3/4 cups vegetable stock
400ml/1 3/4 cups coconut milk
1 pinch sea salt

Ingredients for paste

2 lemon grass stalks
2 garlic cloves, peeled
3 red chillies
5 cm fresh ginger root, peeled
4 kaffir lime leaves
1 lime, juiced

Ingredients for serving

1 tbsp fresh mint
1 tbsp coriander leaves
Small cucumber, chopped, deseeded

Method

1. Preheat the oven to 200C/400F/Gas Mark 6. Sprinkle the beetroots with 1 tablespoon of vegetable oil and season with sea salt. Wrap them in kitchen foil, place in a roasting tray and roast for 35 minutes until tender. Cool, peel and chop.

2. For the paste, peel the tough outer coating from the lemon grass stalks. Finely chop the white bulbous part of each stalk, discarding the rest.

3. Put the lemon grass, garlic, chillies, ginger, kaffir lime leaves and lime juice in a blender. Blend until smooth.

4. Cook the pasta, and combine with the soup mixture, then serve.

Italian Tortellini Soup (Serves 2)

Ingredients

1 large onion (chopped)

3 cloves garlic (minced)

4 carrots (peeled and sliced)

2 stalks celery (sliced)

200g/1 1/2 cups cheese-filled tortellini

150g/1 cup red kidney beans (rinsed and drained)

200ml/1 cup chicken broth

2 medium-sized courgettes (sliced)

4 tomatoes (chopped)

1 tsp dried thyme (crushed)

Grated Parmesan cheese (optional)

Method

1. Place the onion, carrots, celery, garlic, thyme and 2 cups broth in a large saucepan. Heat to a boil.

2. Cover and cook over a low heat for 10 minutes or until onion is tender. Add the remaining chicken broth, courgette, tomatoes, tortellini and beans.

3. Heat to a boil, reduce heat and cover. Cook for 15 minutes or until tortellini is al dente.

Serve with grated Parmesan cheese and bread if desired.

Beef & Macaroni Soup (Serves 2)

Ingredients

350g/3 cups extra lean ground beef
80g/1/2 cup elbow macaroni
450g/3 cups tomatoes (chopped)
450g/3 cups kidney beans (drained)
2 1/2 cups beef broth
1/2 tsp onion powder
1/2 tsp garlic powder
1 1/2 tsps Italian seasoning

Method

1. In a large saucepan, cook the ground beef over a medium heat until browned, for about 5 minutes, stirring occasionally.

2. Drain the beef in a colander, then transfer to a large plate lined with paper towels. Blot the beef with additional paper towels, and then return the beef to the saucepan.

3. Mix in the broth, Italian seasonings, onion and garlic powders. Cover and bring to a boil.

4. Integrate the macaroni, then return to the boil, and reduce the heat. Cover and simmer until the macaroni is just tender, about 9 minutes.

5. Stir in the tomatoes and kidney beans. Return to the boil to heat through, before serving.

Minestrone Soup (Serves 2-4)

Ingredients

950ml/4 1/2 cups vegetable stock
800g/6 cups stewed tomatoes
2 stalks celery (chopped)
1 large potato (cubed)
1 onion (chopped)
1 large courgette (sliced)
2 carrots (chopped)
1 large head cabbage (finely chopped)

400g/2 3/4 cups kidney beans
460g/3 1/2 cups fresh corn kernels
200g/7 oz uncooked pasta of your choice
1 tsp Italian seasoning
Salt and pepper to taste

Method

1. In a large soup pot, combine the vegetable stock, tomatoes, potato, onion, celery, carrot, cabbage and Italian seasoning. Bring to a boil and reduce the heat. Simmer for 10 minutes.

2. Next, stir in the beans, corn, zucchini and pasta, and then simmer for 15 more minutes until the vegetables are tender. Season with salt and pepper.

Pasta Fagioli (Serves 2-4)

Ingredients

2 cups cooked elbow macaroni
450g/3 cups kidney beans (undrained)
1 clove garlic (minced)
1 large onion (chopped)
700g/1 lb 12 oz tomatoes (chopped)
225ml/1 cup tomato sauce
2 tbsps freshly chopped parsley
2 tbsps olive oil
1 tsp salt
1/2 tsp pepper
1/2 tsp dried leaf basil (crushed)
Grated Parmesan cheese

Method

1. Heat the olive oil in a large pan. Sauté onion and garlic until onion is tender and golden, which will take approximately 5 minutes.

2. Add the tomatoes, tomato sauce, salt, pepper, oregano and parsley. Bring to the boil. Reduce the heat, cover, and then simmer for 25 minutes.

Pasta Fagioli/cont.

3. Add the cooked macaroni (cook as per packet instructions beforehand) and beans to the tomato mixture, stirring well. Simmer for 5 minutes, or until thoroughly heated.

Serve in bowls with a sprinkling of fresh Parmesan cheese, or serve the cheese on the side.

Creamy Chicken Pasta Soup (Serves 2-4)

Ingredients

100g/1 cup penne pasta
2 boneless chicken fillets (chopped)
1.6ltr/6 cups chicken stock
100g/3 1/2 oz button mushrooms (sliced)
100g/1 cup celery (sliced)
2 medium carrots (finely chopped)
1 medium onion (chopped)
3 tbsps plain flour
3 tbsps fresh lemon juice
3 tbsps butter
2 tbsps chopped fresh parsley

Method

1. Melt the butter in a large pan over a medium heat. Add the mushrooms, celery, carrots and onion. Cook until celery and onion are tender, about 5 minutes.

2. Add the flour and cook for 3 minutes, stirring occasionally. Gradually mix in the chicken stock. Bring soup to simmer, stirring frequently.

3. Add the chopped parsley and simmer for 5 minutes. Add chicken pieces and simmer until cooked through, for 4-5 minutes.

4. Cook penne pasta in large pot of boiling salted water until al dente. Drain the pasta and bring the chicken soup to simmer.

5. Mix in cooked pasta and simmer 2 minutes. Mix in lemon juice, then season to taste with salt and pepper.

Ravioli Slow-Cook Stew (Serves 2-4)

Ingredients

260g/2 cups sliced carrots
1 onion, chopped
2 cloves garlic, minced
750ml/3 cups vegetable broth
800g/1lb 12 oz tomatoes, undrained
400g/14 oz cannellini beans
1 tsp dried basil leaves
1/4 tsp pepper
300g/11 oz ravioli
1/2 cup grated Parmesan cheese

Method

1. Combine all of the ingredients except ravioli pasta and Parmesan cheese in your slow cooker. Cover, and cook on low for 6 hours until carrots are tender.

2. Increase the heat to high and stir in the ravioli. Cover again and cook for 8 minutes, or until the ravioli are tender.

Sprinkle with cheese and serve.

Turkey Meatball Soup (Serves 2)

Ingredients

2 turkey fillets, chopped
1 tsp salt
1/2 tsp ground pepper
4 sachets chicken broth
450ml/2 cups water
6 tomatoes (diced)
3 carrots (peeled and thinly sliced)
1 celery stick (sliced)
1 medium onion (chopped)
75g/1/2 cup uncooked alphabetti spaghetti
200g/1 1/2 cups red kidney beans (rinsed and drained)

Turkey Meatball Soup/cont.
Method

1. In a medium bowl, combine turkey pieces, salt, and pepper. Roll mixture into 1-inch balls. Set aside.

2. In a large saucepan, bring broth, water, tomatoes, carrots, celery, and onion to a boil. Stir in meatballs. Reduce heat to medium-low and simmer, partially covered, for 50 minutes.

3. Meanwhile, cook alphabet spaghetti according to package directions, and then drain. Simmer spaghetti in soup, for 5 minutes, then stir in the beans.

Lemon Chicken Soup (Serves 4)
Ingredients

2 skinless chicken breasts
1.8 litres/8 cups water
200g/1 1/2 cups ziti pasta
2 eggs
2 lemons
Salt to taste
Ground black pepper to taste

Method

1. In a large soup pot, cook chicken in water until the meat begins to fall off the bone.

2. Skim the fat off the stock. Remove the chicken from pot, and set aside to cool. Add pasta to stock, and cook for about 10 minutes, then shut off heat.

3. In a medium bowl, beat 2 eggs with the juice of 2 lemons until foamy. Whisk 1 cup of stock slowly into the egg/lemon mixture. Repeat with another cup of stock, and pour mixture into soup.

Add the meat to the soup. Stir well. Add salt and pepper to taste.

Wild Mushroom & Pasta Soup

Ingredients

50g/1/3 cup dairy free margarine
1 medium sized onion, chopped
100g/1 cup pasta of choicee
1 clove garlic, crushed
250g/2 cups mixed wild mushrooms, sliced eg. oyster, shiitake
50g/1/2 cup plain flour
600ml/3 cups vegetable stock
Salt and freshly ground black pepper
2 tbsps freshly chopped tarragon
300ml/1 1/2 cups soya milk

Method

1. Melt the margarine in a large saucepan and fry the onions and garlic for 3-4 minutes until softened.

2. Add the mushrooms to the pan and fry for a further 5 minutes until tender. Stir in the flour and cook for 1-2 minutes.

3. Gradually add the stock, stirring continuously. Stir in 1 tablespoon of tarragon. Bring slowly to the boil, then reduce the heat and simmer for 10-15 minutes.

4. Allow the mixture to cool slightly, then puree in a food processor or blender. Rub through a sieve. Just before serving add the milk or cream, season and reheat, without boiling.

5. Cook the pasta until al dente, and then add to soup mixture.

6. Pour into bowls and sprinkle over the remaining tarragon.

Chilli-Prawn Noodle Soup
Ingredients
100g/1 cup rice noodles
1 medium onion, finely chopped
2 spring onions, roughly chopped
1 clove garlic, finely chopped
2 tsps medium curry powder
1 green chilli, finely chopped
2 lemon grass stems, crushed
1 tbsp coriander stalks, crushed
75g creamed coconut
400ml/1 3/4 cups water
200g/1 1/2 cups raw tiger prawns, shelled
500ml/2 1/4 cups chicken stock
50g spinach leaves
4 tsps Thai fish sauce, nam pla
2 tbsps coriander, roughly chopped

Method

1. Cook the noodles following pack instructions and refresh under cold water. Heat the oil in a saucepan and fry the onion, spring onion, garlic, curry powder and chilli for 1-2 minutes.

2. Add the lemon grass, coriander, creamed coconut, water, prawns and stock and simmer for 5 minutes.

3. Add the spinach leaves, and nam pla and simmer for a further minute. Before serving add the chopped coriander, and remove the lemon grass and coriander stalks.

Chilled Rocket & Pesto Soup
Ingredients
1kg/2 1/4lb ripe tomatoes, roughly chopped
1 green pepper, deseeded and roughly chopped
1 onion (chopped)
2 cloves garlic (crushed)
3 tbsps wild rocket pesto
150g/1 cup pasta of your choice

Method

1. First place the tomatoes, green pepper, onion and garlic in a large bowl. Add 2 tbsp of pesto and mix thoroughly. Then leave to marinate overnight, or for at least 8 hours, to let the flavours combine and deepen.

2. The next day place the tomato mix into a processor and process until smooth and season with salt and pepper.

3. Cook the pasta until al dente, and combine with other ingredients. Finally serve in bowls and drizzle with the remaining pesto.

Spicy Lentil Soup

Ingredients

500g/3 cups brown lentils
1.4 litres/6 cups vegetable stock or water
2 bay leaves
A small bunch of finely chopped parsley
salt and fresh ground black pepper
2 tbsps olive oil
1 medium onion, chopped
1 head of garlic, chopped
2 carrots, finely chopped
1 small tomato, chopped
Half a red pepper, chopped
2 tsps sweet paprika
1 tbsp ground cumin
50g/1/3 cup rice
50ml/1/4 cup Manzanilla sherry

Method

1. Place the lentils in a large saucepan. Add the stock or water, bay leaves and parsley. Bring to the boil, reduce the heat, season with salt and freshly ground pepper and simmer, partly covered.

2. Meanwhile, heat the olive oil in a frying pan. Fry the onion gently until softened, around 5 minutes.

Spicy Lentil Soup/cont.

3. Add the garlic, carrot, tomato and red pepper. Fry gently for 5 minutes. Remove from direct heat, season with salt and freshly ground pepper, paprika and cumin.

4. Add the onion mixture and the rice to the simmering soup. Simmer the soup until the lentils are tender, around 45 minutes in all. Mix in the sherry and serve.

My Recipe

Ingredients:

Chicken Taglatelly
Taglatelly Pasta
chicken Breasts
single cream
salt and Black pepper
spinich Leaves

Preparation:

My Recipe

Ingredients:

Preparation:

My Recipe

Ingredients:

Preparation:

My Recipe

Ingredients:

Preparation:

My Recipe

Ingredients:

Preparation:

My Recipe

Ingredients:

Preparation:

My Recipe

Ingredients:

Preparation:

My Recipe

Ingredients:

710 mL / 3 cups warter
225 g / 1 cup seashell paster
235 mL / 1 cup whole fat milk
450 g / 2 1/4 cups shedded chees 80 g

Preparation:

My Recipe

Ingredients:

Preparation:

My Recipe

Ingredients:

Preparation:

My Recipe

Ingredients:

Preparation:

My Recipe

Ingredients:

Chicken and Bacon Pasta

Preparation:

Pasta Bows
4 rashers of Bacon
Brocoley
DuBBle creem
2 chicken Thies
ovioil
Garlic clove
Ground Black Pepper
Chedder cheese.

INDEX

The recipes contained in this book are passed on in good faith but the publisher cannot be held responsible for any adverse results. Please be aware that certain recipes may contain nuts. The recipes use both metric and imperial measurements, and the reader should not mix metric and imperial measurements. Spoon measurements are level, teaspoons are assumed to be 5ml, tablespoons 15ml. For other measurements, see chart below. Times given are for guidance only, as preparation techniques may vary and can lead to different cooking times.

Spoons to millilitres

1/2 teaspoon	2.5 ml	1 Tablespoon	15 ml
1 teaspoon	5 ml	2 Tablespoons	30 ml
1-1 1/2 teaspoons	7.5 ml	3 Tablespoons	45 ml
2 teaspoons	10 ml	4 Tablespoons	60 ml

Grams to ounces

10g	0.25oz	225g	8oz
15g	0.38oz	250g	9oz
25g	1oz	275g	10oz
50g	2oz	300g	11oz
75g	3oz	350g	12oz
110g	4oz	375g	13oz
150g	5oz	400g	14oz
175g	6oz	425g	15oz
200g	7oz	450g	16oz

Metric to cups

Description			
Flour etc	115g	1 cup
Clear honey etc	350g	1 cup
Liquids etc	225ml	1 cup

Liquid measures

5fl oz	/4 pint	150 ml
7.5fl oz		215 ml
10fl oz	1/2 pint	275 ml
15fl oz		425 ml
20fl oz	1 pint	570 ml
35fl oz		1 litre